Dinosaur
Search

Rob Waring, *Series Editor*

THOMSON

HEINLE

T0354108

Australia · Canada · Mexico · Singapore · United Kingdom · United States

Words to Know

This story is set in Niger, which is a country in Africa. It happens in the Sahara [səhɑːrə] Desert.

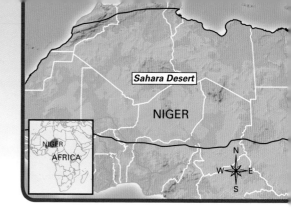

 Parts of a Dinosaur. Read the sentences. Write the number of the correct underlined word next to each item in the picture.

1. The shoulder girdle joins the body and the arms or front legs.
2. The pelvis joins the body and the back legs.
3. The limbs are the arms and legs of a body.
4. The jaw is the lower part of the face that moves when the mouth opens.

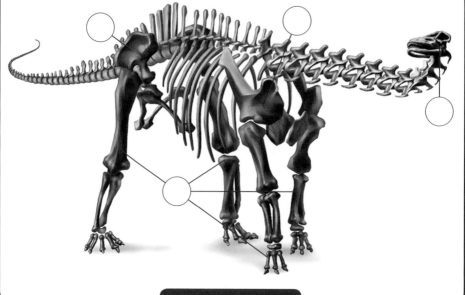

A Dinosaur Skeleton

B Fossils in the Desert. Look at the pictures and read the paragraph. Then complete the paragraph with the words in the box.

bones	fossils	prehistoric
desert	palaeontologist	sand

Dinosaurs are (1)_____ animals. They lived long before people documented history. The scientists who study them are called (2)_____. These scientists often study dinosaur (3)_____, or the hard parts inside the body. They also study animal and plant parts that have been saved in rock. These are called (4)_____. In this story, a team of scientists looks for dinosaur parts in the (5)_____. The dry air there helps save the dinosaur bones. However, sometimes the (6)_____ covers up the bones so they are difficult to find.

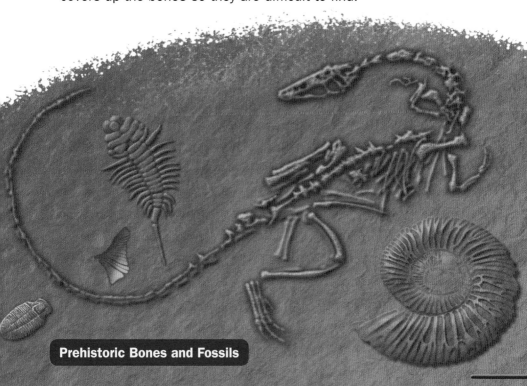

Prehistoric Bones and Fossils

The Sahara Desert is also known as Africa's dinosaur **graveyard**.[1] The Sahara is one of the best places to look for the bones of prehistoric animals. It's a place that has many **secrets**.[2] Some of these secrets have been hidden under the sand for hundreds of millions of years. Now, a team of scientists is searching for these secrets.

---

[1]**graveyard:** an area of land where dead bodies are found under the ground
[2]**secret:** something no one knows about; something hidden

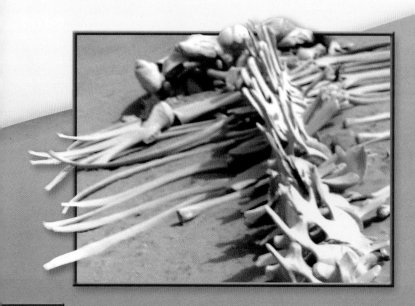

Palaeontologist Dr. Paul Sereno and his team are in the Sahara looking for **clues**.[3] They hope that these clues will lead them to dinosaur bones. These bones may help them to better understand dinosaurs and the time period in which they lived. Dr. Sereno explains: "We're **on the trail of**[4] a number of dinosaurs. We begin to **paint a much better picture**[5] of this time [period] each time we come [to the Sahara]."

The team drives across the desert. Then suddenly, one of the team members says, "Hey! Back there!" The team stops to look around the area. They're near the right place.

---

[3]**clue:** a sign or information that helps to solve a problem or answer a question
[4]**on the trail of:** following; trying to find
[5]**paint a better picture (of something):** get a better understanding or image of something

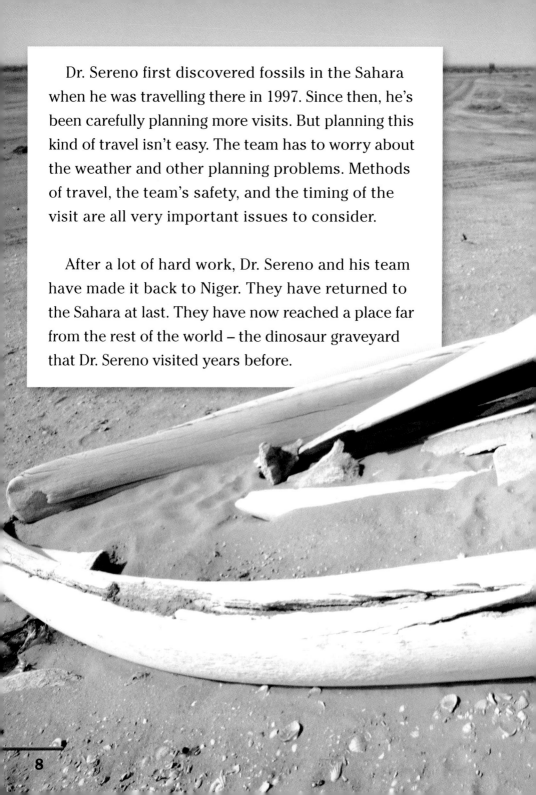

Dr. Sereno first discovered fossils in the Sahara when he was travelling there in 1997. Since then, he's been carefully planning more visits. But planning this kind of travel isn't easy. The team has to worry about the weather and other planning problems. Methods of travel, the team's safety, and the timing of the visit are all very important issues to consider.

After a lot of hard work, Dr. Sereno and his team have made it back to Niger. They have returned to the Sahara at last. They have now reached a place far from the rest of the world – the dinosaur graveyard that Dr. Sereno visited years before.

Scan for Information

Scan page 8 to find the information.

1. When did Dr. Sereno first discover fossils in the Sahara Desert?

2. What problems do Dr. Sereno and his team have when visiting the Sahara Desert?

3. Where is the team now?

Now that the team is in the correct place, the dinosaur search can begin. There are bones everywhere in this dinosaur graveyard.

It doesn't take the team a long time to discover them. They talk about the bones as they find them. "It's part of a shoulder girdle," says one team member, as he picks up a bone. Another team member finds something else. "It's a **distal end**[6] of a limb bone right there," he says as he points to the end of a bone. And another: "We've got what looks like a leg."

Nearby, there's another discovery. "Hey look at this!" says one member. "It's a pelvis!" However, as another team member comes closer to see the bone, he gets in trouble. "Wait, you're stepping on it!" says the team member who found it. Everyone needs to be very careful with these prehistoric bones and fossils.

---

[6]**distal end:** part farthest away from where something is attached

The dinosaur search continues. The team finds bones from several prehistoric animals. They have collected a lot of **promising**[7] fossils, and are very happy about it. Unfortunately, life isn't so good for the team in other ways.

The desert is a hot place, and the team has used up most of their water. They are now worried because the water truck hasn't arrived yet. "After today, we'll have a day and a half's worth of water," says one team member. "We're just hoping for the water truck to get here in time," he adds. Luckily, it does!

Their water worries are over, and there's one more thing they don't have to worry about…

---

[7] **promising:** likely to be very good or helpful in the future

… and that's finding enough fossils! The team makes one important discovery after another. They carefully document each find.

Then, one day as they are walking around, they make their biggest discovery yet; they find the jaw of the prehistoric crocodile sometimes called 'super croc'! This discovery is big – very big – and the jaw bone is in very good condition.

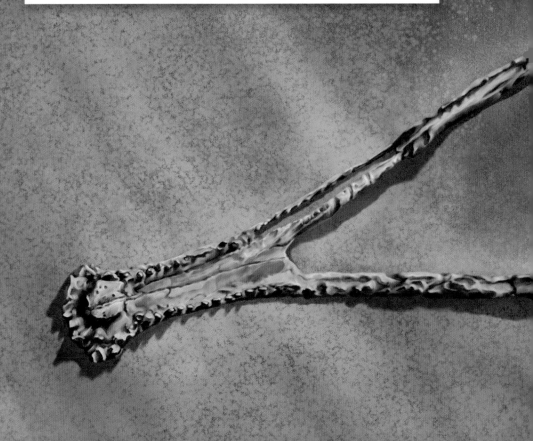

The palaeontologists make a big discovery.

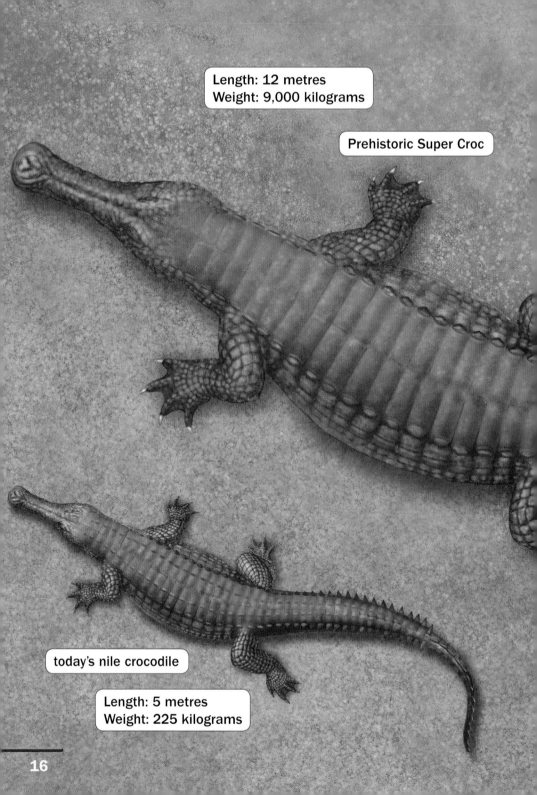

Length: 12 metres
Weight: 9,000 kilograms

Prehistoric Super Croc

today's nile crocodile

Length: 5 metres
Weight: 225 kilograms

In fact, the discovery of the jaw bone is so important that the team soon gets a visit. National Geographic crocodile expert Brady Barr comes to the work site. Barr looks at the super croc bones with Dr. Sereno as they talk about the super croc. This ancient animal was very, very large. It was far bigger than the crocodiles that live today. The questions that scientists have about super croc are big too. What did it look like? What did it eat? How did it **hunt**?[8]

---

[8]**hunt:** catch and kill animals for food

Brady Barr and Dr. Sereno can't answer these questions yet. However, they do realise that they probably won't find the answers in the desert sand. They will probably find them in the **swamp**.[9] Studying the crocodiles of today may tell these experts even more about the 110 million year old bones.

The palaeontology team has made a great discovery on this dinosaur search. However, now that they have found these bones, a new search – one for more information – must now begin.

---

[9]**swamp:** area of very wet, soft land; crocodiles often live there

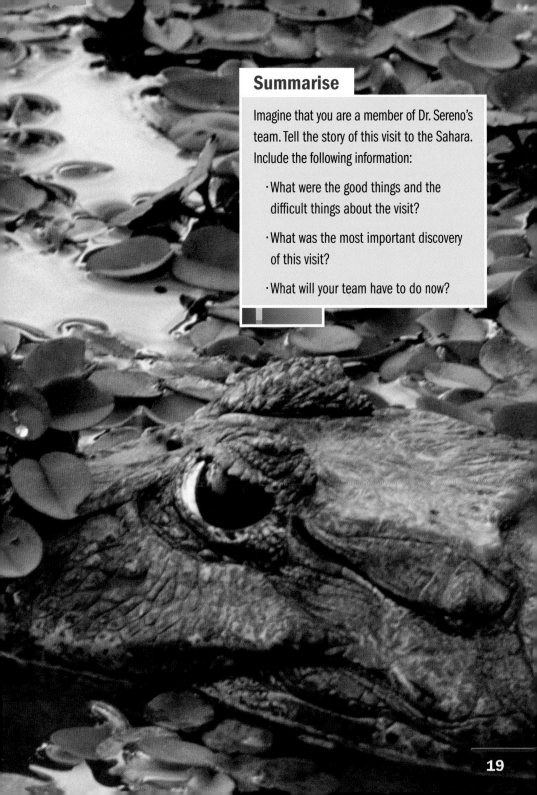

Summarise

Imagine that you are a member of Dr. Sereno's team. Tell the story of this visit to the Sahara. Include the following information:

- · What were the good things and the difficult things about the visit?

- · What was the most important discovery of this visit?

- · What will your team have to do now?

After You Read

1. On page 4, the word 'team' can be replaced by
   A. test
   B. researchers
   C. group
   D. class

2. In the Sahara Desert, secrets have been hidden _____ many years.
   A. while
   B. for
   C. in
   D. under

3. On page 7 'them' in 'will lead them' refers to:
   A. bones
   B. clues
   C. dinosaurs
   D. palaeontologists

4. Dr. Sereno thinks the bones can teach us about:
   A. painting
   B. history
   C. trails
   D. palaeontologists

5. Weather, safety, and timing are all important considerations for the team's visit.
   A. True
   B. False

6. What is a good heading for the second paragraph on page 8?
   A. Team Arrives at Fossil Site
   B. Graveyard Close to Home
   C. Sereno Comes To Visit Often
   D. Team Leaves the Sahara

7. What's the main purpose of page 11?
   A. To show that the team is unsure about the bones.
   B. To show that the team is never careful.
   C. To show that there are different types of dinosaur bones.
   D. To teach about different kinds of fossils.

8. The best heading for page 12 is:
   A. Team Only Has Success
   B. Team Has Success But Faces Problems
   C. Only Problems With Visit
   D. Water Never Arrives

9. The team uses _____ all their water.
   A. just
   B. almost
   C. might
   D. maybe

10. On page 14, the verb 'document' means:
   A. to record
   B. to think
   C. to refer
   D. to decide

11. What's significant about the super croc discovery?
   A. The importance of the discovery.
   B. The size of the fossil.
   C. The good condition of the fossil
   D. all of the above

12. Why is the answer in the swamp?
   A. Because the sand is too deep.
   B. Because the swamp is very old.
   C. Because they must study living crocodiles.
   D. Because the rest of the bones are there.

DINOSAUR
Discoveries

Dinosaur Eggs

Palaeontologists know that dinosaurs grew and developed inside eggs. These eggs were hard and they protected the young dinosaurs. The process is similar to how birds grow and develop nowadays. However, dinosaur eggs are different from bird eggs. The outside of a dinosaur egg is much heavier. Dinosaur eggs are also a lot bigger than bird eggs. Dinosaurs created special places to keep their eggs safe and warm called 'nests'. Birds also build nests for their eggs. Most birds build their nests in trees. However, prehistoric dinosaurs built their nests on the ground. Interestingly, palaeontologists think that dinosaurs covered their nests with dead plants to keep the eggs warm. A few of today's birds also do this.

Dinosaur Eggs

Dinosaur Footprints

Dinosaur footprints range in size – some are very small and some are very large. These footprints were made millions of years ago when the ground was soft and wet. Later on, sand filled the footprints. As time passed, this earth and sand turned into stone and the footprints remained in the stone. Nowadays, palaeontologists can tell a lot from dinosaur footprints. For example, the depth of the footprint helps them to understand how heavy the dinosaur was. Recently, palaeontologists have discovered lots of footprints going in the same direction. This means that dinosaurs probably travelled together in large groups.

Dinosaur Footprints

Dinosaur Fossils

The best dinosaur fossils were formed when three things happened in a very short period of time. First, the dinosaur died. After that, the soft parts of the dinosaur went into the earth. The dinosaur bones remained on the ground. Finally, the bones and dinosaur parts were covered by sand before any were lost or broken. Palaeontologists study fossils to learn about dinosaurs. They are always searching for new fossils. However, it is not always easy to find them. Fossils are usually discovered in two ways. Sometimes the wind wears the earth away. This makes it easier for palaeontologists to spot new fossils. Other times fossils are uncovered by workers preparing to build a new road or building.

Word Count: 335
Time: _____

Vocabulary List

bone (3, 4, 7, 11, 12, 14, 17, 18)
clue (7)
desert (3, 4, 7, 9, 12, 18)
distal end (11)
fossil (3, 8, 9, 11, 12, 14)
graveyard (4, 8, 11)
hunt (17)
jaw (2, 14, 17)
limb (2, 11)
on the trail of (7)
paint a better picture (of something) (7)
palaeontologist (3, 7, 15, 18)
pelvis (2, 11)
prehistoric (3, 4, 11, 12, 14, 16)
promising (12)
sand (3, 4, 18)
secret (4)
shoulder girdle (2, 11)
swamp (18)